THE MOON

Robert Louis Stevenson

THE MOON

pictures by Denise Saldutti

A Harper Trophy Book

Harper & Row, Publishers

Library of Congress Cataloging in Publication Data
Stevenson, Robert Louis, 1850–1894.
   The moon.

   Summary: Illustrations portray a father and
daughter going fishing against a background of
Stevenson's poem about nightly happenings in
the light of the moon.
   1. Children's poetry, English. [1. Moon—
Poetry. 2. Night—Poetry. 3. English poetry]
I. Saldutti, Denise, ill. II. Title.
PR5489.C52   1984   821'.8   83-47704
ISBN 0-06-025788-1
ISBN 0-06-025789-X (lib. bdg.)
ISBN 0-06-443098-7 (pbk.)

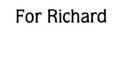

For Richard

The moon has a face like the clock in the hall;

She shines on thieves on the garden wall,

On streets

and fields

and

harbor quays,

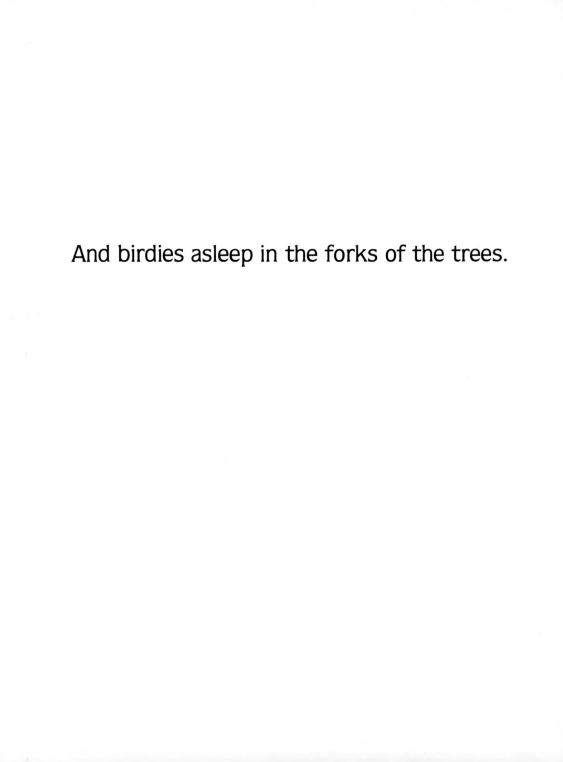

And birdies asleep in the forks of the trees.

The squalling cat

and the squeaking mouse,

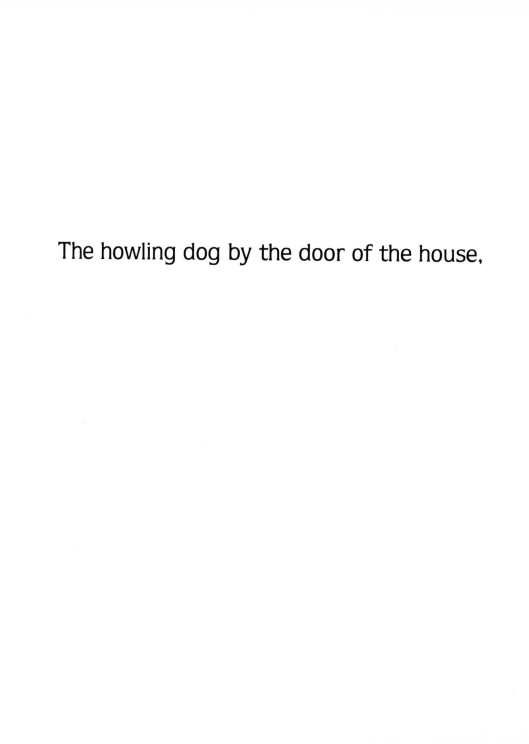

The howling dog by the door of the house,

The bat that lies in bed at noon,

All love to be out by the light of the moon.

But all of the things that belong to the day

Cuddle to sleep to be out of her way;

And flowers and children close their eyes

Till up in the morning

the sun shall arise.